Crossing the Bridge Between You and Me

Friendship-building Devotions for Today's Busy Woman

Discovery House
PUBLISHERS

BOX 3566 · GRAND RAPIDS, MI 49501

PUBLISHING BOOKS THAT FEED
THE SOUL WITH THE WORD OF GOD.

Unless otherwise indicated, Scripture is taken from the Holy Bible: New International Version (North American Edition). Copyright © 1973, 1978, 1984 by the International Bible Society. Used by permission of Zondervan Bible Publishers.

Library of Congress Cataloging-in-Publication Data
Lenzkes, Susan L.
    Crossing the bridge between you and me : friendship-building devotions for today's busy woman.
      p. cm.
    ISBN 0-929239-83-0
    1. Friendship—Religious aspects—Christianity—Meditations. 2. Women—Religious life. I. Title.
    BV4647.F7L46   1994
    242'.643—dc20   94-42539
                                    CIP

Discovery House Publishers is affiliated with Radio Bible Class, Grand Rapids, Michigan.

Discovery House books are distributed to the trade by Thomas Nelson Publishers, Nashville, Tennessee 37214.

Printed in the United States of America

94 95 96 97 98 99 / CHG / 10 9 8 7 6 5 4 3 2 1

To Nancee

God created the harmony in our hearts and let it overflow in song.
I thank God for the gift of a precious friend like you!

But God didn't stop there.
He made me fabulously wealthy with . . .
Betty, Carol, Dolores, Judi, Judy, June,
Marlene, Martene, Mary, and Sandee,
each a treasure of love and loyalty, each a time-tested, beloved friend.
How I look forward to spending eternity together with you!
And with my **Mother,** *my lifetime friend,*
who already waits there for me.
Then there is **Herb,** *my dearest friend and husband.*
How I thank God for restoring you to my arms
for whatever time He allows.
And to **Cathy, Jeff,** *and* **Matt**
I no longer call you children, but friends!

All praise and thanks to the Friend above all friends,
Jesus Christ, my Savior and Lord.
Grateful thanks to the many dear ones at Discovery House
who have prayed for me, for my family, and for this book.
I am honored by the friendship of publishers
Bob DeVries and Carol Holquist,
committed friends of God who
continuously demonstrate His love.
Special appreciation to Julie Ackerman Link
for insight, skill, and supportive friendship.
Eternal thanks to the many friends
who have lifted me and my beleaguered family
in prayer as I have written this book. God bless:
our family at Vista Grande Church,
the women's Bible study group,
neighbors and nearby friends,
the G.R.A.C.E committee in Roseburg, Oregon,
friends in the Christian Writer's Guild of San Diego County,
my brothers and sisters and Dad,
prayer chains all around the country,
and those friends who are far from us in distance
but near in our hearts. I love you all.

Introduction

It's *easy to get spoiled* in this fast-paced, high-tech, instant-everything world. Compute it quick. Fax the facts. Microwave the dinner. Call from your car. Reach for the remote. Speed dial. Laser print. Jet to Jamaica.

But there's no place that can fax you a friend. To get a friend, you have to build a bridge. And even with modern technology, bridge-building is a process that takes time. There is no shortcut that can span the distance between two hearts.

Building solid, close relationships is critically important. And if your life is anything like mine I don't need to tell you why you need friends. Every days is filled with reasons!

How could we keep our balance in this stress-filled world without the perspective of a friend? How would we grow and learn and find hope when we're running low? Who would laugh with us at the end of a day when laughing seems the only thing left to do? Who would share our joys? How would we survive our successes and learn from our failures? Who would lift us when we're sinking beneath our load? And who would hug us when life turns out to be full of pain? Who would share our tears?

Is it time for you to work on a bridge or two?

Need a Friend?

After the friendship of God, a friend's affection is the greatest treasure here below.
—Unknown

If you're feeling like an only child . . .

If your laughter has no home and your tears no shoulder . . .

If you've forgotten how to run through the grass in your bare feet . . .

If you've run out of patience and need to borrow some . . .

If your tea bag is only half used . . .

If you have love to give away . . .

If there's a victory to celebrate . . .

If you can see one side of a problem very clearly . . .

If you could use a safe deposit box for deep hurts and confidences . . .

*If you're certain the sun will never come out
  again . . .*

If everyone else has walked away . . .

*If you need someone able to see and hear with her
  heart . . .*

*If a mirror would help you to get a good look at
  yourself . . .*

If eating alone is no fun . . .

*If you need a helping hand, a pat on the back, or
  a swift kick . . .*

*If you're looking for an honest answer wrapped
  with kindness . . .*

If you've fallen down and skinned your knee . . .

If you don't know who to call for prayer . . .

If a hug would help . . .

*If you need someone who needs you right
  back . . .*

*If you want to live a longer, happier, healthier
  life . . .*

*Then you need a **friend**, my friend!*

*Perfume and incense bring joy to the heart, and the
pleasantness of one's friend springs from his [her] ear-
nest counsel.*   —Proverbs 27:9

A friend loves at all times, and a brother is born for adversity.   —Proverbs 17:17

Your love has given me great joy and encouragement.
                                        —Philemon 7

The Priority of Friendship

Above all, love each other deeply.
—1 Peter 4:8

Friends *are such* a delight that they sometimes seem to be a luxury—a reward for getting everything else done. But as we run from the urgent to the imperative and back again, many of us find that we don't get around to this "luxury" often enough—though we intend to.

Building friendships might even strike us as self-indulgent. Friends are called "flowers for the heart" and "a gift we give ourselves." Perhaps we think the heart can survive without flowers and presents.

Is friendship just a lovely extravagance God provides to fill our leisure hours and enhance our enjoyment on this earth? Many of us will never invest the time or take the risk of building lasting bridges to others until we're convinced that close relationships are an essential, not an extra.

Today's medical experts are discovering the remarkable value of good relationships. Their studies reveal that people who have friends are *healthier*, physically as well as psychologically. They have even found that those with close companions tend to *live longer* than people who are isolated and lonely. Further, they tell us that when we make it through crisis situations we can credit the *support system around us* more than our own strength of character.

Good, practical reasons for developing enduring friendships.

But for those of us who have been born into God's family through Christ, our authority for the importance of building relationships is our Lord's example and His Word. Throughout the Bible we hear His persistent call for love and unity. When a teacher of the law asked Jesus which was the most important commandment, Jesus said nothing was more important than the command to love God and others (Mark 12:28–31).

Jesus' years of ministry on earth leave little doubt that loving others and investing time and energy in their lives was His number one priority—more important than earning an income, owning a house, or living to retirement age.

He chose twelve common men and loved them so effectively that He turned them from sinners into servants and finally into friends of God. Together they fished, ate, walked, talked, worked, celebrated, slept, understood, taught, traveled, cried, rejoiced, and grew. And many others, including numerous women, followed Jesus, helping, learning, and becoming disciples and cherished friends. He made friends of criminals, outcasts, the poor, the wounded, and the sick as well as the wealthy, healthy, religious, and influential.

Christ's love for others was, and still is, redemptive, healing, helping, and life-saving. In Him, our love for one another can be the same. But for that, we must be as committed in building bridges of love to one another as Christ was in building His bridge to us.

"My command is this: Love each other as I have loved you. Greater love has no one than this, that he lay down his life for his friends. You are my friends if you do what I command. I no longer call you servants, because a servant does not know his master's business. Instead, I have called you friends, for everything that I learned from my Father I have made known to you. You did not choose me, but I chose you and appointed you to go and bear fruit—fruit that will last. Then the Father will give you whatever you ask in my name. This is my command; Love each other."

—John 15:12–17

"I pray also for those who will believe in me through their message, that all of them may be one, Father, just as you are in me and I am in you. May they also be in us so that the world may believe that you have sent me. I have given them the glory that you gave me, that they may be one as we are one: I in them and you in me. May they be brought to complete unity to let the world know that you sent me and have loved them even as you have loved me."

—John 17:20–23

Building Bridges

In my opinion developing open relationships is the best way to survive on this lonely, busy planet, and it is worth whatever risk it requires . . . to build bridges to one another.
—Charles R. Swindoll, *Dropping Your Guard*

"We *don't build* bridges the way they used to, you know," the owner of the structural steel bridge building company said, responding to my query about how to build a bridge.

"Sir," I said, "you're assuming I know how they *used* to do it!"

"I see," he chuckled. "Well, they used to just build them a piece at a time. But not any more! Now we truck huge pre-fabricated hunks of a bridge to the site and eventually weld them together into a bridge."

What a graphic picture of relationships in our society!

People used to grow up together in small communities where friendships were built gradually, simply, and naturally . . . a day at a time. People actually *knew* one another—sharing their fears, joys, struggles, losses, and dreams—often from birth to death. But not anymore!

In today's crowded and mobile society many of us truck huge pre-formed hunks of ourselves from place to place, then discover the need to somehow weld ourselves to our new neighbors in some sort of bridge to span our isolation. Previously developed parts of our personalities—attitudes, bents, customs, temperaments, needs, hopes, perceptions—remain separated from other people. Our wounds are covered, our dreams guarded. And we are unfamiliar with the techniques required to build modern-day bridges of friendship. We are even unsure where to begin.

"How," I asked my bridge-building expert, "do they hold all those big pieces together until they can be joined by welding?"

"Have you ever driven down the highway and seen a bridge under construction that looks like it has *scaffolding* all around it?" he asked. "Well, that's called *shoring*. Shoring is the temporary structure that we build to hold everything together until it can be welded into place."

What will "shore us up" as we try building bridges to one another? What supports our relationships until our lives and hearts can be welded together in love?

Fortunately we serve a God who is able to bring us together and hold us together. In so many healthy, creative ways, He continually draws us into relationship with Himself, and with one another. In God's Word we learn that the Father, Son, and Holy Spirit are One; that God sent His Son to die and rise again to conquer sin and restore our relationship with Him; that Jesus declared His followers no longer servants, but friends; and that God is creating a family for Himself, and we are brothers and sisters in Christ.

So it is God's loving example and gracious provision for building such unity that becomes our "shoring." We need to deliberately surround ourselves with His supportive truth until His way of loving becomes part of who we are.

Most of us find ourselves in the position of needing to *work* at building the kind of friendships that once came naturally in small, close communities with common values. We need to consciously do those things that Christ modeled for us, things that let us be known to others and that, in turn, help us to know and understand them. We need to bridge our fears and deal with our reticence, practicing honesty, openness, acceptance, availability, and non-judgmental support. We need to rediscover how to laugh, love, share, care, and grow together.

But take heart. Such bridge-building can be fun and exciting. And one day, as we become bonded in love, that shoring will come down and we'll find ourselves running back and forth across a beautiful bridge of friendship that spans all the way to eternity.

Be completely humble and gentle; be patient, bearing with one another in love. Make every effort to keep the unity of the Spirit through the bond of peace. There is one body and one Spirit—just as you were called to one hope when you were called—one Lord, one faith, one baptism; one God and Father of all who is over all and through all and in all. . . . Speaking the truth in love, we will in all things grow up into him who is the

Head, that is, Christ. From him the whole body, joined and held together by every supporting ligament, grows and builds itself up in love, as each part does its work. —Ephesians 4:2–6, 15–16

And so we know and rely on the love God has for us. God is love. Whoever lives in love lives in God, and God in him. In this way, love is made complete among us. . . . We love because he first loved us. And he has given us this command: Whoever loves God must also love his brother. —1 John 4:16–17, 19, 21

See that what you have heard from the beginning remains in you. If it does, you also will remain in the Son and in the Father. And this is what he promised us—even eternal life. —1 John 2:24–25

Worth the Risk

If we build more windows and fewer walls we will have more friends.
—Alan Loy McGinnis, *The Friendship Factor*

When *we trust* another person enough to tell her who we really are and how we really feel, we have shared our most precious possession. But for many of us, such openness seems like the ultimate risk. We feel vulnerable. What if we are taken lightly, belittled, betrayed, rudely corrected, abandoned, or rejected? Painful experiences flash their warning light within us, *Danger! Do not enter!*

Such fears can give us a healthy sense of caution about indiscriminately stripping bare our soul to total strangers, or to people who have not shown themselves to be trustworthy. From such experiences we can learn the wisdom of a gradual process of discovery and disclosure.

But caution has gone beyond discretion when it keeps us closed off from others, living in fear of revealing who, what, and where we are. For not only is it healthy, right, and good to know and be known as we go through life, but there will inevitably come a time when we desperately need the ministry of someone who already understands and loves us.

One day I was sitting on the floor, working on a project with a friend. She seemed unusually quiet and withdrawn. Sensing trouble and not wanting my friend to suffer an internal explosion that could do serious damage when there would be no one around to administer first aid, I began to gently probe. At my subtle inquiries, she dodged and slid sideways, so I let it go and we continued our work.

During a break, I leaned against the wall, drew my legs to my chest, rested my chin on my knees, and began to share an area of need that could have made me vulnerable to her judgment. She listened with empathy, expressed her support, and finally said,

"You shared that with me so that I'd be able to talk about what's wrong, didn't you?"

"Who, *me?*" I laughed, and then grew serious as her pain tumbled out in a heartrending torrent.

Later her world fell apart, and I will never forget what she said. "I'm so glad I shared with you before. I don't have to explain anything now. You already know. You see, I *couldn't* explain anything now. I'd have been *alone* in this . . . "

Through openness, we had built a bridge of friendship that she could run across in a crisis—run to understanding, comfort, caring, and help. In an emergency is no time to start a building project.

Keep on living an open, transparent life, because that is where the Spirit blooms and produces fruit in authentic relationships and demonstrates the kind of life God approves.

As we continue to share honestly with each other, we help one another grow to our full potential as Christpersons in unity with Christ our head. As each of us stays in union and harmony with Christ, we are energized and consequently give energy to others through Christ, enabling them in their growth and giving love to the family as a whole.

Discover new ways of expressing your new, unique personhood in Christ, ways which are in harmony with who you really are. This new behavior will demonstrate that you have a right relationship with yourself and with God and are becoming a whole person. Stop playing games, and be straight in your communication, because we are all dependent on each other.

—Ephesians 5:8–10, 4:15–16, 24–25

Scripture taken from *The Heart of Paul, A Relational Paraphrase of the New Testament*, by Ben Campbell Johnson.

Neighboring Souls

Better a neighbor nearby than a brother [or sister] far away.

—Proverbs 27:10

A *friend is*
 the soul's close neighbor,
one from whom
 we borrow freely
 a pound of laughter,
 a teaspoon of advice,
 a cup of encouragement,
 a loaf of love.
I'm so glad the
gate between us is
always open.

As much as is possible, friends need to be available to one another. It takes time to beat a path from one heart to another—time spent laughing, talking, listening, and helping. But if we begin feeling that we must be there in every need, available in every crisis, we could use a reminder that there is only one Friend capable of that.

Once I was conducting an important meeting in my home when the phone rang. It was a friend urgently in need of a listening ear. Quietly I said, "I have a house full of people here right now, so I can't talk. But you know that I care. I love you, and I'll call you back as soon as this meeting's over."

When I returned her call she said, "Thank you for taking time to say you care and to remind me of your love. You can't know how much it meant to hear that at that moment. And thank you for saying you'd call back—and then doing it. But a funny thing happened. When you weren't available, I went to my knees and had a very precious time with the Lord. I'm okay now."

What a wonderful reminder that, whether through us or around us, it is always and only our Lord who meets needs. He is there when we are and when we aren't. How precious when He slips through the gate and down the path to a friend's heart, quietly embracing needs in His arms of sufficiency.

> *Praise be to the God and Father of our Lord Jesus Christ, the Father of compassion and the God of all comfort, who comforts us in all our troubles, so that we can comfort those in any trouble with the comfort we ourselves have received from God.*
> *—2 Corinthians 1:3–4*

> *Each of us should please his neighbor for his good, to build him up. May the God who gives endurance and encouragement give you a spirit of unity among yourselves as you follow Christ Jesus, so that with one heart and mouth you may glorify the God and Father of our Lord Jesus Christ.   —Romans 15:2, 5–6*

A Firm Foundation

On Christ, the solid Rock, I stand—All other ground is sinking sand.
> —Edward Mote, *The Solid Rock*

"What do you consider to be the most important principle of bridge building?" I asked.

There was a thoughtful pause before the bridge-builder answered. "To build a bridge you must have good solid abutments and foundation." He slowed, adding emphasis to his next words. "Because no matter how strong the steel, a bridge is only as good as its foundation."

Foundational truth remains consistent throughout creation, I realized. God's laws for building solid structures apply just as surely to building solid relationships. A friendship, too, is only as good as its foundation.

On what can we build our bridges of friendship? Is there any solid ground? Is there anything or anyone we can really count on?

Must we place our hope on the shifting sands of psychology's most recent theory, or in someone's passing affection, promises of convenience, or conditional love? Even the most ardent declarations and the best intentions and efforts of others can fade and fail.

We live in a fallen world, and sin struck first and hardest at relationships, shattering the bridge of perfect union between God and those He created in His likeness. That same sin brought mistrust, greed, competitiveness, betrayal, manipulation, resentment, and fear, which carve a chasm between humans.

But there is good news. Built into the foundations of the world was the Cross of Christ—our bridge back to the faithful, unconditional love of God. When we build our relationships on the solid rock of Jesus Christ, we are safe. What a Friend we have in Jesus!

Each one should be careful how he builds. For no one can lay any foundation other than the one already laid, which is Jesus Christ. —1 Corinthians 3:10–11

"*Therefore everyone who hears these words of mine and puts them into practice is like a wise man who built his house on the rock. The rain came down, the streams rose, and the winds blew and beat against that house; yet it did not fall, because it had its foundation on the rock. But everyone who hears these words of mine and does not put them into practice is like a foolish man who built his house on sand. The rain came down, the streams rose, and the winds blew and beat against that house, and it fell with a great crash.*"
—Matthew 7:24–27

So this is what the Sovereign Lord says: "*See, I lay a stone in Zion, a tested stone, a precious cornerstone for a sure foundation; the one who trusts will never be dismayed.*" —Isaiah 28:16

Quality Material

A righteous man [woman] is cautious in friendship.

—Proverbs 12:26

All materials used to build a bridge, I am told, must pass rigid inspection because a quality bridge requires quality material. And a quality friendship requires quality people.

Who and what I am, and who and what you are, combines to create the unique bridge between us. Our friendship is as delightful or dull, as solid or fragile, as simple or complex, and as good or bad as we are.

In light of this, the quality of my personality and especially that of my character, take on new importance. What I bring to our relationship will affect you deeply as our experiences combine to create "us." What you bring to my life affects me just as much.

This gives us a sense of caution, for we realize that we could never pass close inspection—that, left to ourselves, we could never be the high-quality material to consistently build good into the lives of others. For we know our weaknesses, failings, and shortcomings.

But we rejoice to find that we are offered new life in Christ, and as we stay close to Him, His holy, winsome, wonderful character is formed in us. When we share the love and life of Christ we build solid, beautiful, eternal bridges between ourselves and others.

Do not be yoked together with unbelievers. For what do righteousness and wickedness have in common? Or what fellowship can light have with darkness?
—2 Corinthians 6:14

Therefore, if anyone is in Christ, he is a new creation; the old has gone, the new has come! All this is from God, who reconciled us to himself through Christ and gave us the ministry of reconciliation: that God was reconciling the world to himself in Christ, not counting men's sins against them. And he has committed to us the message of reconciliation. We are therefore Christ's ambassadors, as though God were making his appeal through us. We implore you on Christ's behalf: be reconciled to God. God made him who had no sin to be sin for us, so that in him we might become the righteousness of God.   —2 Corinthians 5:17–21

Cutting Remarks

Do not use a hatchet to remove a fly from your friend's forehead.
—Chinese Proverb

Some people seem to confuse exhortation with extermination. As they see it, their spiritual gift is insight into other people's problems. Their motto is, "The truth never hurt anyone." And their rationalization is, "What are friend's for?" They waste no time in slashing through ignorance and denial to get to the heart of things.

But before allowing someone to cut into us at a point where we are already wounded, it is wise to find out if she has earned her surgeon's license. Is this person operating on the law of love? It takes extensive education and experience to know how to cut someone up for her benefit. And it takes selfless, tender, faithful, sacrificial love.

Sometimes an operation is advisable, or even urgently needed to save a life. Only in those cases will a caring surgeon encourage a patient to surrender to the scalpel and endure the pain. Cancerous tumors, hidden away in the body, destroy. Sin, covered over and denied, destroys.

It seems, however, that many friends are performing unnecessary surgery these days. This may be due to an error in diagnosis. Often they just don't have all the facts. At other times the surgery seems to benefit the one wielding the knife more than the one beneath it (if I can just change the shape of that nose she'll look like a Christian is *supposed* to look!).

We need to check our motives, our wisdom, and our license before attempting the quick fix of sharp truth. We may find we're simply dealing out pokes, digs, cuts, and jabs. Too many people are hiding scars left by impatient friends who couldn't tolerate the slower, more natural ways to wholeness—ways costly in time, attention, prayer, and caring.

Needles and knives are safest in the hands of our Great Physician.

> "Why do you look at the speck of sawdust in your brother's [sister's] eye and pay no attention to the plank in your own eye? How can you say to your brother [sister], 'Let me take the speck out of your eye,' when all the time there is a plank in your own eye? You hypocrite, first take the plank out of your own eye, and then you will see clearly to remove the speck from our brother's [sister's] eye."
>
> —Matthew 7:3–5

> Brothers [sisters], if someone is caught in a sin, you who are spiritual should restore him [her] gently. But watch yourself, or you also may be tempted. Carry each other's burdens, and in this way you will fulfill the law of Christ.   —Galatians 6:1–2

> "A new command I give you: Love one another. As I have loved you, so you must love one another. By this all men will know that you are my disciples, if you love one another."   —John 13:34–35

The Bridge of Forgiveness

He that cannot forgive others, breaks the bridge over which he himself must pass if he would ever reach heaven; for every one has need to be forgiven.

—George Herbert

The potential for misuse is inherent within every bridge of friendship. Jesus knew this all too well. He also seemed to know that His friends would frequently wrong one another, so He sat them down and outlined the steps for rebuilding the bridge when one party damaged it through abuse or neglect.

He explained that the first step was for the offended friend to privately point out the problem to the offending friend. Hopefully that would be enough. If not, he or she was to take two others along and try again. If even that failed, they were to enlist the help of the church. If the person failed to renounce his or her sin after this extreme measure, then and only then, they were to let the person go (implying that a reckless, unrepentant person is a danger to the openness required of true love.)

Apparently Peter thought this sounded like a lot of trouble and got to wondering how many times he'd be required to go through such a difficult process. So he pulled Jesus aside and suggested an upper limit of seven—surely a generous number under the circumstances.

But Jesus was into "higher math" and told Peter he had to forgive his brother "not seven times, but seventy times seven!" Perhaps Peter walked away astounded at the number of offenses that his brothers could inflict upon him, never realizing that Jesus may have been suggesting that he might need to forgive a brother that many times for a single serious offense.

When trust has been violated, forgiveness is seldom a one-step process—especially if the relationship is to be restored. Close friendship has a built-in vulnerability because through it we allow another person to know the best and worst that we are. When trust is broken in such a relationship, we run hard against the need to forgive, often again and again, as each new opportunity to trust presents itself. Complete forgiveness is a process that unfolds in layers of fresh affirmation.

As difficult as this is, and even though much prayer and wisdom must surround and guide us, it is only as God leads us to transparently trust once again that full healing and restoration can be brought to a relationship.

In forgiving and inclining ourselves to the repentant one who has wronged us, we follow God's amazing example. When God sent His Son to us, we disregarded, abused, and finally killed Him. Yet as we confess our sin He not only forgives us, He dares to entrust this same beloved Son to live within us!

It is this Friend who promises never to leave or forsake us (though He knows our failings and weakness). He is the Friend who says that if we confess our sins He will forgive our sins. It is this wonderful Friend who teaches us that when we forgive others (however many times it takes) we are merely passing along the favor of His redemptive grace.

"If your brother sins against you, go and show him his fault, just between the two of you. If he listens to you, you have won your brother over. But if he will not listen, take one or two others along, so that every matter may be established by the testimony of two or three witnesses. If he refuses to listen then, tell it to the church; and if he refuses to listen even to the church, treat him as you would a pagan or a tax collector."

—Matthew 18:15–17

Then Peter approached and said to him, "Lord, how often shall my brother act amiss toward me and I forgive him? Up to seven times?" Jesus said to him, "I do not say, up to seven, but up to seventy times seven."

—Matthew 18:21–22 MLB

For if you forgive others their trespasses, your heavenly Father will forgive you too; but if you do not forgive people, neither will your heavenly Father forgive your trespasses.

—Matthew 6:14–15 MLB

Bear with each other and forgive whatever grievances you may have against one another. Forgive as the Lord forgave you.

—Colossians 3:13

Reflections

**As water reflects a face, so a man's [woman's]
heart reflects the man [woman].**
—Proverbs 27:19

I sat
and looked,
really looked,
at me
in the mirror.
Would I want to be
my friend
if I were someone else?
Would I tire of the
shape
of that face,
of the expressions it wore?
Would I see twinkling eyes

and warm smiles
often enough?
Would I look into those
dark eyes and
know
I could share
anything?
Could I trust those lips
to stay gentle,
not thin and judging?
And the tongue—
would it be
still
beneath the weight of
secrets?

Let us examine our ways and test them, and let us re-
turn to the Lord. —Lamentations 3:40

The lamp of the Lord searches the spirit of a man
[woman]; it searches out his [her] inmost being.
—Proverbs 20:27

Test me, O Lord, and try me, examine my heart and my mind; for your love is ever before me, and I walk continually in your truth. —Psalm 26:2–3

And we, who with unveiled faces all reflect the Lord's glory, are being transformed into his likeness with ever-increasing glory, which comes from the Lord, who is the Spirit. —2 Corinthians 3:18

A Covered Bridge

To be a "safe place" for others, I must have an open heart and a closed mouth.

I *have a friend* who is for me like a cozy covered bridge—a sheltered place where I can wander until I'm ready to run in confidence, where I can test new thoughts and unfamiliar feelings.

Having come often to this cherished "safe place," I realize there is no gift more precious than that of understanding.

This friend has steadily and clearly reflected who, what, and where I am in my journey through life. I find that I have been joined—though never intruded upon—in this journey of discovery and growth.

When I thank God for His rich goodness toward me, I thank Him for this friend. And when I ask God to make me like His Son Jesus, and to use me in His kingdom and for His glory, I feel Him making me into a safe place, an understanding place, a steady, warm, non-judgmental, and, oh yes, a leak-proof place—like this friend.

The wise in heart are called discerning, and pleasant words promote instruction. Understanding is a fountain of life to those who have it . . .
—Proverbs 16:21–22

The purposes of a man's [woman's] heart are deep waters, but a man [woman] of understanding draws them out. —Proverbs 20:5

Each man [woman] will be like a shelter from the wind and a refuge from the storm, like streams of water in the desert and the shadow of a great rock in a thirsty land. —Isaiah 32:2

Genesis Moment

This day you have become the people of the Lord your God.
> —Deuteronomy 27:9 MLB

Everything in life has its
   "genesis moment"—
that bridge of a moment when
   what wasn't, suddenly
      is.
Praise God for the moment
   when you
spanned that bridge into my life—
   for the moment that birthed
      our friendship.

He who created the heavens, he is God; he who fash-
ioned and made the earth, he founded it; he did not
create it to be empty, but formed it to be
inhabited . . .   *—Isaiah 45:18*

For he chose us in him before the creation of the
world.   *—Ephesians 1:4*

He has made everything beautiful in its time. He has
also set eternity in the hearts of men; yet they cannot
fathom what God has done from beginning to end. I
know that everything God does will endure forever;
nothing can be added to it and nothing taken from it.
God does it so that men will revere him.
                              —Ecclesiastes 3:11, 14

Shout for joy to the Lord, all the earth. Worship the
Lord with gladness; come before him with joyful songs.
Know that the Lord is God. It is he who made us, and
we are his; we are his people, the sheep of his pas-
ture.   *—Psalm 100:1–3*

He [she] who walks with the wise grows wise . . .
                              —Proverbs 13:20

The Art of
the Heart

Whoever draws a smile upon a weary soul is God's artist.

Encouragement *is* one of God's most joyous art forms. He supplies us with the raw materials and invites us to create, build, and shape His hope in the lives of those around us.

Some people combine a helping hand with a word of praise and produce a grateful heart. Others, by mixing laughter and love, are able to paint new sparkle in dulling eyes. Belief and support build self-esteem. Persistent prayer composes a song of hope; and tenderness and warm embraces fashion a friend.

However we combine the elements of encouragement, one thing we're sure to create is joy—for others, for ourselves, and for our Lord.

I want to be able to do something about your joy: I want to make you happy, not sad.
                              —2 Corinthians 1:24 TLB

My mouth would encourage you; comfort from my lips would bring you relief.   —Job 16:5

Therefore encourage one another and build each other up, just as in fact you are doing.
                              —1 Thessalonians 5:11

It Takes More than One

Jesus' home was the road along which he walked with his friends in search of new friends.
—Giovanni Papini

Sometimes *we place* an unrealistic and unfair burden on a loved one, spouse, or friend. That one person is expected to meet all, or nearly all, of our relational needs. No one on earth is capable of that. Only of God can it be said, "He is all I need."

When it comes to human relationships, we are wise to build more than one "bridge" between ourselves and others. A look at Jesus' life reveals that He made a variety of friends while walking this earth. His friendships crossed cultural, economic, and gender barriers. He even seemed to have different friends for different needs.

He had *working friends*—disciples and followers who learned, labored, and ministered alongside Him. Through much of their three years together Jesus stood shoulder-to-shoulder with these friends, working with them toward a common goal.

It appears, however, that when Jesus really wanted to get away from it all, He went to his *resting friends*—Mary, Martha, and Lazarus. With these friends He would most often sit face-to-face, visiting, eating, and relaxing. Basking in their loving hospitality, he was renewed and refreshed.

Are most of your friends the kind who work shoulder-to-shoulder with you? Do you have no one to whom you can go for heart-sharing and renewal? Or perhaps you have a friend with whom you sit face-to-face and share your heart and hopes, but this person is rarely there to help you shoulder burdens and reach goals.

Maybe you have many working and sharing friends, but few with deep, intimate understanding.

Even among His twelve chosen friends, Jesus had a particularly close bond with Peter, James, and John.

Perhaps it is time to begin building a few new bridges.

> *Now about brotherly love we do not need to write to you, for you yourselves have been taught by God to love each other. And in fact, you do love all the brothers . . . yet we urge you, brothers, to do so more and more.* —1 Thessalonians 4:9–10

The Rx for Laughter

A cheerful heart is good medicine.
—Proverbs 17:22

"*It's been rough,*" my friend said, "but I've finally made it through!" We were celebrating the completion of a miserable, but necessary, year of chemotherapy treatment in her battle against cancer.

She leaned back and looked at me thoughtfully. "You'll never know how much I appreciated all those cards, notes, and letters you sent to me day after day."

I laughed and told her that she *should* appreciate them since I'm usually the world's most inconsistent letter-writer. But I explained that God had assigned me "mailbox duty" that year. And along with the assignment He gave me an unusual sense of eagerness and joy about it, so if the letters had helped she should thank *Him*.

"Well, the love and encouragement kept me going," she said. "But do you know what I appreciated more than anything else in those letters? Those funny, silly things you wrote that made me *laugh*. Because at a time like that, just when it's most needed, laughter is the hardest to find."

Truly, laughter is a gift that we can give to one another—a gift meant to be shared. Laughter, joy, and just plain fun have a way of building strength into friendships. Laughter creates memories. It is life's bubbles and often its best medicine. And strips of shining laughter weave friendship's basket tight enough to hold the tears.

A happy heart makes the face cheerful, but heartache crushes the spirit. All the days of the oppressed are wretched, but the cheerful heart has a continual feast. A cheerful look brings joy to the heart, and good news gives health to the bones.

—Proverbs 15:13, 15, 30

However many years a man [woman] may live, let him [her] enjoy them all. But let him [her] remember the days of darkness, for they will be many.

—Ecclesiastes 11:8

I know that there is nothing better for men [women] than to be happy and do good while they live.

—Ecclesiastes 3:12

Lend Me an Ear

**It is impossible to over-emphasize the immense
need humans have to be really listened to.**
—Paul Tournier

Ears are busy these days. A listening, caring, available
ear is increasingly difficult to find. Many seem perma-
nently encased in the headphones of their own pri-
vate interests. Others are busy vying for equal time
with other parts of the body—such as an eye on the
clock or a nose to the grindstone.

Even a free ear isn't necessarily free just to listen.
When people come to us with their troubles, many of
us discover we have a birth defect; our earbone is
connected to our mouthbone. When patience,

understanding, and encouragement are most needed, we give advice, platitudes, and "My experience can top *that*" stories.

The burdened who come to us needing to unburden are looking for an earbone connected to a heartbone.

If anyone has an ear, let him hear.
                              —Revelation 13:9

My dear brothers, take note of this: Everyone should be quick to listen, slow to speak.   —James 1:19

He who answers before listening—that is his folly and his shame.   —Proverbs 18:13

A man of knowledge uses words with restraint.
                              —Proverbs 17:27

What Did I Expect?

A real friend has no strings, no binding precon-
ceptions, no limiting agendas . . . The bond of
love releases people.
—Lloyd John Ogilvie

If *we dared to unwrap* and examine the feelings we
have for those closest to us, I suspect that many of us
would find a somewhat mixed package. Not only do
we cherish our loved ones for who and what they are,
but also for what we need them to be.

This hidden "wish list" affects our relationships
with family members, friends, and, probably most
often, the one to whom we are married. Unacknowl-
edged and unexplored expectations can frustrate, dis-

appoint, and tie us in knots. They prove to be even more frustrating to the person who fails to match our dreams.

Most of us have not consciously entered our close relationships with preconceived notions. Yet each of us has grown up with a unique set of hopes, fears, and perceptions that have shaped our longing for the "ideal friend" or "perfect partner." Such desires and aspirations may have created a natural affinity for the heart of a particular kind of person, leading us toward our choice of friends or mate.

Inevitably, these people prove to be who they are, not who we thought they were or who we wanted them to be. Our level of frustration and disappointment reveals our hidden expectations.

In healthy relationships we share our hearts and lives, but sometimes we forget that we cannot expect another person to fix our brokenness or fill in where someone else failed us. Sometimes the wishful heart forgets that no one outside of Christ can meet all of our needs or fulfill all of our hopes for security, love, perfect understanding, and unfailing loyalty.

Occasionally we even discover that we have written our own hidden definitions of how love should prove itself. Our expectations scrawl deep longings in a language read constantly by the finger-tips of our feelings—assessing, measuring, evaluating. "If she cared she wouldn't be so busy . . ." "If he loved me he would know how I feel . . ." "If she were a real friend she'd call more often . . ." or "he'd buy me gifts . . ." or "she wouldn't criticize me . . ." or "he'd always ask how my day went."

Such assumptions don't always voice themselves. They are recurring feelings of neglect, disappoint-ment, or disapproval that create great unhappiness for us.

And when we allow our expectations to define the worthiness of our loved one, we create great unhappiness for him or her. If he doesn't understand or express his emotions like I do, then clearly, some-thing is wrong with him. Since she doesn't think or act the way I do, she's not just different, she's defi-cient. We may even begin to manipulate others, seeking to change them into people who are better suited to meet our needs.

Yet if we are to be good, true, and righteous friends, we will not seek to refashion one another to meet our expectations. We will be careful not to accept one another with only our heads and our mouths, while nourishing disapproval in our hearts.

Instead, each of us will loose our dreads and dreams in open sharing. We will speak our needs, content to let them rest lightly in the hand and heart of our loved one. Then we will see what God and we can do, together.

I expect great things of honest friends.

Teach me your way, O Lord, and I will walk in your truth; give me an undivided heart . . .
—Psalm 86:11

The wisdom of the prudent is to give thought to their ways. —Proverbs 14:8

All a man's [woman's] ways seem right to him [her], but the Lord weighs the heart. —Proverbs 21:2

Search me, O God, and know my heart; test me and know my anxious thoughts. See if there is any offensive way in me, and lead me in the way everlasting.
—Psalm 139:23–24

So from now on we regard no one from a worldly point of view. Therefore, if anyone is in Christ, he is a new creation; the old has gone, the new has come! All this

is from God, who reconciled us to himself through
Christ and gave us the ministry of reconciliation . . .
—2 Corinthians 5:16–18

Where the Spirit of the Lord is there is freedom.
—2 Corinthians 3:17 RSV

Increase in Value

Formerly he was useless to you, but now he has become useful both to you and to me.
—The Apostle Paul (Philemon 11)

Onesimus was a slave, quite possibly a renegade who had stolen from his master, Philemon. He seemed to be of little worth—until the apostle Paul befriended him. From his prison cell Paul shared the good news of the love of Christ with this runaway, and God's love dramatically increased his value. Suddenly this slave became "my son . . . very dear to me . . . useful . . . a dear brother . . . my very heart" (Philemon 10–16).

Do you know people who feel and act as though they aren't worth much . . . people enslaved by sin, bad habits, weakness, or self-loathing? We who carry the love of God within us have the power to increase their value from useless to useful, from slave to dear brother or sister. This is the joyous privilege of friendship in Christ.

I appeal to you for my son Onesimus, who became my son while I was in chains. I am sending him—who is my very heart—back to you. Perhaps the reason he was separated from you for a little while was that you might have him back for good—no longer as a slave, but better than a slave, as a dear brother. He is very dear to me but even dearer to you, both as a man and as a brother in the Lord. So if you consider me a partner, welcome him as you would welcome me. If he has done you any wrong or owes you anything, charge it to me. —Philemon 10, 12, 15–18

Little
Lifts

**The best relationships are built up, like a fine
lacquer finish, with the accumulated layers of
many acts of kindness.**
—Allen Loy McGinnis, *The Friendship Factor*

The size of a deed is measured not so much by its effort
as its impact.

My husband, an early riser, often wakens me, a
night owl, by placing a steaming mug of coffee on my
night stand. Such a small thing, but it makes me feel
so cherished and pampered.

A friend regularly jots me a note of love, appreciation, or encouragement. How can one thin piece of
paper lift me so high?

Another friend makes a quick phone call that manages to warm my whole day. My son passes by and stops to rub the weariness from my shoulders, and this time he doesn't even want anything! A neighbor calls out a cheery greeting that lingers. A stranger passing on the sidewalk dares to look me in the eyes and smile.

A brother from church sees me carrying a heavy load and says, "Here, let me."

A "hello" comes enveloped in a hug.

Someone says, "You look wonderful in that color," or "What you shared helped me," or "I missed you yesterday," or "I was praying for you this morning," or "Come share my sandwich."

Someone warms my heart with a contagious laugh; a toddler shyly presses a damp M&M into my hand; my daughter shares a secret; someone unexpected remembers my birthday with a card and note; a friend calls and says, "Quick, go look at the sunset"; my sister touches my hand with unspoken understanding; a friend says, "Try again, I know you can do it."

These are the things that brighten and lighten life. These are the little things that make a big difference. They're not expensive, difficult, or time-consuming. They're just appreciated, remembered, and so vitally important. They're each day's small building blocks of love.

"Who despises the day of small things?"
                                    —*Zechariah 4:10*

Do good . . . be rich in good deeds . . . be generous and willing to share.   —*1 Timothy 6:18*

And whatever you do, whether in word or deed, do it all in the name of the Lord Jesus, giving thanks to God the Father through him.   —*Colossians 3:17*

Hug
Power

**I often tell people it doesn't take great wisdom to
energize a person, but it does take sixty seconds.
That's the amount of time it takes to walk over
and gently hold someone we love.**
　　　　—Gary Smalley, *Love Is a Decision*

If *someone started* selling stock in hugs, I'd mortgage
my house and invest everything. Hugs are indispensable. They're the shape of a full heart, the feel of love.
They're as useful in good times as they are in bad
(they're as good at celebrating as they are at comforting!) And they're used as freely in greetings as in farewells—not to mention all the times in between.

Hug experts even claim that people must have a minimum daily requirement of hugs for the maintenance of health and sanity. Sounds right to me! I credit hugs with great power.

Hugs speak love and understanding without uttering a sound.

A hug is especially valuable in times of trouble. On some days a friend's gentle hug is the only pressure the wounded heart can bear.

I like hugs because they squeeze shut the space between hearts. For a moment our aloneness is wrapped up in someone else—a blanket against isolation.

But Esau ran to meet Jacob and embraced him; he threw his arms around his neck and kissed him. And they wept. —Genesis 33:4

So Joseph brought his sons close to him, and his father kissed them and embraced them. —Genesis 48:10

[Jesus] took a little child and had him stand among them. Taking him in his arms, he said to them . . . "Whoever welcomes a little child like this welcomes me." —Mark 9:36, Matthew 18:5

Feeling
at Home

Make room for us in your hearts.
—2 Corinthians 7:2

Certain friends have a way of
setting up residence in us.
They march into some
barren room of our heart and
hang cheery curtains,
scatter soft rugs,
dot the walls with framed prints of
tender and whimsical moments,
then set about building a
cozy fire beside two
sink-back-and-stay-awhile chairs.
We may not always know exactly when

such friends moved in,
but we're so very glad they did!

Some people have a way of making themselves at home. They don't ring the front doorbell. They slip in the back with a freshly plucked daisy or two. No formalities. Just, "How wonderful to see you!"

They don't care if there's clutter on the floor. They'll either help you pick it up, or step over it to pour you each a cup of coffee. "A penny for your thoughts," they say. "No, a nickel; your thoughts are always worth more."

How do these people do it? Perhaps the key to the back door of our hearts is simply *acceptance*—the kind of love that would just as soon hug you in a tattered bathrobe as in your Sunday best. Such people leave behind their expectations of how others should be and what they should do. To them, every person is buried treasure to be discovered and enjoyed. Differences are a source of delight. Evaluations, judgments, and makeovers are not their job. Loving acceptance is.

When such a person takes me into her heart, it is certain that she cannot stay long out of mine.

"It is right for me to feel this way about all of you, since I have you in my heart. —Philippians 1:7

Accept one another, then, just as Christ accepted you, in order to bring praise to God. —Romans 15:7

Be devoted to one another in brotherly love. Honor one another above yourselves. Live in harmony with one another. Do not be proud, but be willing to associate with people of low position. Do not be conceited. —Romans 12:10, 16

Now that you have purified yourselves by obeying the truth so that you have sincere love for your brothers, love one another deeply, from the heart. For you have been born again, not of perishable seed, but of imperishable, through the living and enduring word of God. —1 Peter 1:22–23

I Love You Because

. . . sometimes you hug instead of talk.

. . . your appointment book is filled with people, not things.

. . . I'm never just one more thing in your crowded day.

. . . I don't have to change or improve to please you.

. . . the time you spend loving God shines in your eyes.

. . . you spread enthusiasm like peanut butter between thick slices of bread.

. . . you turn moments into memories.

. . . when you laugh you enjoy it (and so does everyone else!).

. . . *you constantly draw others into your circle of warmth.*

. . . *your vulnerability lets me know I'm not alone.*

. . . *'flat on your face' is merely a temporary position for prayer and napping.*

. . . *you hear with your heart.*

. . . *you are a leak-proof repository.*

. . . *my burdens go from your heart directly into God's hands.*

. . . *you wait with me for God's deliverance in His timing.*

. . . *you know not only what love is, but what it does.*

. . . *you draw talents from people that they didn't even know they had.*

. . . *just being your friend inspires me to be the best I can be.*

I thank my God every time I remember you. In all my prayers for . . . you, I always pray with joy because of your partnership in the gospel from the first day until now, being confident of this, that he who began a good work in you will carry it on to completion until the day of Christ Jesus. —Philippians 1:3–6

And this is my prayer: that your love may abound more and more in knowledge and depth of insight, so that you may be able to discern what is best and may be pure and blameless until the day of Christ, filled with the fruit of righteousness that comes through Jesus Christ—to the glory and praise of God.

—Philippians 1:9–11

Hand-print Prayers

I want men [and women] everywhere to lift up holy hands in prayer.
—1 Timothy 2:8

I *watched as she* spread her hand on the piece of white paper and then carefully traced around it. I smiled at the big bump where her ring had slipped sideways, and I admired the way her long nails tapered gracefully. Then she put my hand on another piece of paper and handed me the pencil. The tracing around my arthritic knuckles was wide. I didn't like the look of it. Then she wrote her name on her drawing and instructed me to write my name on mine.

I was mystified by this kindergarten art project. We were grown women with grown children; friends of many years, now separated by too many miles. Solemnly she presented her drawing to me, then took mine.

"Now," she said, "we can keep these in our Bibles and pray for one another. Like this." Gently she placed her own warm hand over the empty outline of my hand. "Sort of a long distance way of 'laying on of hands.' It will help us to feel close." Then she added with a smile, "And I will remember to pray for your arthritis."

How I thank and praise God for the ministry of friends who pray with experience, love, and understanding. Such friends may be responsible for more good in our lives than we will ever know this side of heaven.

We are wise, then, to work at being that kind of friend to others. For faithful, fervent, need-specific prayer is one of the greatest gifts we can give.

And such prayer has a way of bringing us close, even when we're far apart. As we lift one another to our heavenly Father with holy hands of prayer, we are united by His Spirit in the bond of love—held together in His righteous hand.

"My Father, who has given them to me, is greater than all; no one can snatch them out of my Father's hand."

—John 10:29

For this reason I kneel before the Father, from whom his whole family in heaven and earth derives its name. I pray that out of his glorious riches he may strengthen you with power through his Spirit in your inner being, so that Christ may dwell in your hearts through faith. And I pray that you, being rooted and established in love, may have power together with all the saints, to grasp how wide and long and high and deep is the love of Christ, and to know this love that surpasses knowledge—that you may be filled to the measure of all the fullness of God. Now to him who is able to do immeasurably more than all we ask or imagine, according to his power that is at work within us, to him be glory in the church and in Christ Jesus throughout all generations for ever and ever! Amen.

—Ephesians 3:14-21

A Real
Friend

A friend is the one who comes in when the whole world has gone out.
—Unknown

I had always heard
that a friend is
there when everyone else
isn't,
believing when everyone else
hasn't,
understanding when everyone else
doesn't,
loving when everyone else
wasn't.
 You iz!

You haz!
You duz!
You wuz! *

*Two are better than one, because they have a good re-
turn for their work: If one falls down, his friend can
help him up. But pity the man who falls and has no one
to help him up! Though one may be overpowered, two
can defend themselves. A cord of three strands is not
quickly broken.*   —Ecclesiastes 4:9–10, 12

*It was good of you to share in my troubles . . . you
sent me aid again and again when I was in need.
And my God will meet all your needs according to his
glorious riches in Christ Jesus.*
                              —Philippians 4:14, 16, 19

*I have great confidence in you; I take great pride in
you. I am greatly encouraged; in all our troubles my
joy knows no bounds.*   —2 Corinthians 7:4

Poem originally published as a DaySpring greeting
card, Outreach Publications. Book rights retained by
Susan Lenzkes.

Practicing Patience

The greatest thing a man can do for his heavenly Father is to be kind to some of his other children.

—Henry Drummond

The little boy didn't seem to know or care that he'd wandered into the intersection. He was preoccupied with a palm branch he was dangling just beyond the reach of each step—a tantalizing target designed to see if his foot could outsmart his hand. The driver who had had to stop in the middle of the intersection and wait out this tedious trek looked toward my car, knowing he was blocking my passage, then threw his hands up in resignation and his head back in laughter.

Dear man, I thought, joining him in laughter, *bless you for your watchfulness, patience, and sense of humor that allows you to help this little one survive his walk home—and even to enjoy him.*

And I thought about all of God's children on their way home: some so young they don't know how to safely cross the street; some rushing and bumping into others; some wounded and running blindly into life's intersections; and some just distracted, preoccupied, playing little games with their feet. How pleasing to the Lord are those willing to brake for the progress of His children—and even to smile about it.

Bear with the failings of the weak. . . . and not to please ourselves. Each of us should please his neighbor for his good, to build him up. —Romans 15:1–2

Dear brothers, warn those who are lazy; comfort those who are frightened; take tender care of those who are weak; and be patient with everyone. See that no one pays back evil for evil, but always try to do good to each other and to everyone else. Always be joyful. Always keep on praying. No matter what happens, always be thankful, for this is God's will for you who belong to Christ Jesus. —1 Thessalonians 5:14–18 LB

No Small Help

Don't let us think that we need to be "stars" in order to shine. It was by the ministry of a candle that the woman recovered her lost piece of silver.

—John Henry Jowett

I *had just been* unceremoniously informed of my shortcomings as a mother. My thwarted and angry preteen had drawn on the full lexicon of his experience and vocabulary to perform the task. His awesome barrage of accusations somehow managed to penetrate my shield of better judgment. I sat nursing wounds in my bedroom and wondering if I might, indeed, somehow hail from the family tree of Frankenstein.

Soon I heard footsteps, both tentative and rushing. The folded paper thrust into my hand was accompanied by only the briefest look into my eyes—a glance of shy, quick compassion—before this youngest son ran back out of the room. He had been a silent witness to my Waterloo with his brother.

I looked down at the paper. "To a great mums!" it read. (He has never called me mums before or since.) Tenderly I unfolded his message and read (creative spelling and all), "I am glad you are my mums because you help me and care for me and show me how to eat the right way." (I noticed he wrote that I'd shown him; he didn't claim that he'd learned!) "You rote a book for mothers who need help" (in which case, I wrote the book for myself!) "and rote the book for money to help us live." (Fortunately, that wasn't my motive!) "You help mothers because you care for others and not onley for yourself. So that proves that your the perfecked mother for just about anyone. Love, Matt, Your Son." (No extra charge for the identification!)

At the bottom of the page was a wonderful drawing of a skinny stick person with long arms stretched out to a typewriter, presumably working on another book to help others—and obviously living off the proceeds!

How precious to find a friend at your side in an hour of need. Is anyone too small or weak to lift sagging spirits with a heartfelt message of love and faith?

An anxious heart weighs a man [or woman] down, but a kind word cheers him [her] up.
                                                                                        —Proverbs 12:25

Pleasant words are a honeycomb, sweet to the soul and healing to the bones. *—Proverbs 16:24*

A word aptly spoken is like apples of gold in settings of silver. *—Proverbs 25:11*

Costly Love

Hugs are delightful—until you meet a porcupine!

How many of us struggle to find ways to embrace "porcupine" people! They can be relatives, neighbors, or co-workers who bristle at the slightest provocation, who needle us constantly with their digs and stabs. Any attempt to reach out or to get close results in painful wounds. Yet dare we stop trying?

The porcupines in our lives need love far more than other people. Their rigid quills are a coverup for surprising vulnerability. They've been hurt by people like us. They're afraid of being hurt again. Quills are their only protection.

It will cost us some of our own blood to get close enough to reach the person beneath the prickles. But can we claim to pick up our cross and follow Christ without sharing His suffering?

But rejoice that you participate in the sufferings of Christ, so that you may be overjoyed when his glory is revealed. . . So then, those who suffer according to God's will should commit themselves to their faithful Creator and continue to do good.

—1 Peter 4:13, 19

Bless those who persecute you; bless and do not curse. Do not repay anyone evil for evil. Be careful to do what is right in the eyes of everybody. If it is possible, as far as it depends on you, live at peace with everyone. Do not take revenge, my friends, but leave room for God's wrath, for it is written: "It is mine to avenge; I will repay," says the Lord. On the contrary: "If your enemy is hungry, feed him; is he is thirsty, give him something to drink. In doing this, you will heap burning coals on his head." Do not be overcome by evil, but overcome evil with good.

Romans 12:14, 17–21

Self-Help

**It is one of the most beautiful compensations of
this life that no man can seriously help another
without helping himself.**
—Ralph Waldo Emerson

When I lift you, my friend,
my arm grows stronger.
When I give to you,
my hand empties to receive.
When I walk with you through
dark valleys,
my feet learn the way to Truth.
When I weep with you,
my eyes wash clear to see
compassion's holy bond.
When I lift you,
I am lifted.

"In everything I did, I showed you that by this kind of hard work we must help the weak, remembering the words the Lord Jesus himself said: 'It is more blessed to give than to receive.'"   —Acts 20:35

He who refreshes others will himself be refreshed.
                    —Proverbs 11:25

You are Precious

As a teacher teaches best by sparking curiosity, so a friend encourages best by kindling self-worth.

Recently a dear friend was talking with me about her struggle to realize her own worth.

"The other day," she said, "I was so frustrated with my slow progress, wondering if I would ever really learn to be kind to myself. Then I thought of you and another friend who have affirmed me for so many years, believing in me even when I didn't honor my own opinions and feelings, and making me feel special when I didn't place much value on myself. And I suddenly understood something that's helping me be more patient with myself.

"I realized that you've loved me a lot longer than I've loved myself, so you're *better* at it! I know where that kind of love comes from. And I know that in time, I'll get better at it too."

What a privilege God has given us to love one another! When the apostle Paul instructed us to observe whatever is true, noble, right, pure, lovely, admirable, excellent, and praiseworthy (Philippians 4:8), he handed us a delightful set of tools to carve self-worth into the lives of others. As we see and affirm these positive qualities in our friends, our friends begin to see the *Source* of all that is true and excellent and praiseworthy. And soon they begin praising their lovely Creator by becoming all He meant for them to be.

> *But now, this is what the Lord says—he who created you . . . he who formed you . . . "Fear not, for I have redeemed you; I have summoned you by name, you are mine . . . You are precious and honored in my sight . . . I love you . . . Forget the former things; do not dwell on the past. See, I am doing a new thing! Now it springs up; do you not perceive it?*
> —Isaiah 43:1–4, 18–19

How great is the love the Father has lavished on us, that we should be called children of God! And that is what we are! This is love: not that we loved God, but that he loved us and sent his Son as an atoning sacrifice for our sins. Dear friends, since God so loved us, we also ought to love one another. No one has ever seen God; but if we love one another, God lives in us and his love is made complete in us.

—1 John 3:1, 4:10–12

The Language of Silence

The language of friendship is not words, but meanings. It is an intelligence above language.
—Henry David Thoreau

I *found myself* awake in the night, rewriting the script of a fumbled opportunity. Earlier that day I had been in a quiet, unhurried place with a dear friend—obvious opportunity to release the bulging safety valve on pent-up pain over a tragic circumstance that we shared.

But I had sent my pain to charm school, so I tried to talk the tears out of my soul in polite little sentences and neatly packaged paragraphs. Now I lay awake acknowledging failure and adding regret to my overload.

Imagination began constructing a second chance. This time I deliberately allowed my questions and my feelings of hurt and loss to speak their own language. I found I was not articulate. There were sudden stops, tear-dampened starts, and halting half-sentences.

Grief's real questions, I realized, have never claimed literacy. Pain and loss are not socialized. Shock stutters. Our deepest feelings are pre-school, even pre-verbal.

Picking up my pen, I shared these fresh understandings with my friend and then added, "As I relived our time together, I finally just imagined myself looking at you—wordlessly and with tears—and you came and hugged me. Wordlessly. With tears. And we held one another's pain without need for explanation.

"I must somehow be overeducated when I cannot set verbiage aside and share feelings properly—naturally. Undereducated is more like it! It has taken me too long to understand that God gave us *words* to communicate our *thoughts*. To communicate our *feelings*, He has given us the common language of *tears*, *laughter*, and *touch*. Sometimes words can be an intrusion—an obstacle.

"I'm so grateful that you're in life's classroom with me, my friend, while I learn how to live better, share better, and become more of what I was created to be.

"Making the grade in this class may mean no more than having the integrity to live appropriately, honestly, genuinely, and openly.

"Stick around. One of these days we may have one of our most meaningful conversations without saying a word! And it will be exactly right, for there is surely a pound of encouragement in every ounce of shared silence."

"In quietness and confidence shall be your strength."
—Isaiah 30:15 KJV

If you have any encouragement from being united with Christ, if any comfort from his love, if any fellowship with the Spirit, if any tenderness and compassion, then make my joy complete by being like-minded, having the same love, being one in spirit and purpose.
—Philippians 2:1–2

Designed
by God

Sometimes I wonder if God said, "Let there be *friends*" at the same moment that He conceived the idea of you and me.

In a million years
I could not have designed
a friend like you.
I might have thought to
give you a smile.
But who, outside of God,
could have added your irrepressible
laughter that
scoops everyone into its joy?
I might have thought to
give you arms.

But who, outside of God,
could have pressed into your curve
a hug that's
just my size?
And I might have thought to
give you a voice.
But who, outside of God,
could have given you voice to say,
"You're always in my prayers"?
Only God could have designed you,
my friend.
How I thank Him for His marvelous works!

For we are God's workmanship created in Christ Jesus
to do good works, which God prepared in advance for
us to do.   —Ephesians 2:10

Let them praise the name of the Lord, for he com-
manded and they were created.   —Psalm 148:5

You are worthy, our Lord and God, to receive glory
and honor and power, for you created all things, and
by your will they were created and have their being.
*   —Revelation 4:11*

O Lord, you are my God; I will exalt you and praise
your name, for in perfect faithfulness you have done
marvelous things, things planned long ago.

—Isaiah 25:1

Bearing One Another's Burdens

When my arms can't reach you, I hug you in my prayers.

Never-ending "pleated prayers"—
rich fabric of a loving heart—
hope folded,
endlessly folded,
over tear stains,
and wrapped like a skirt around
the throne of God.

What a joy it is to pray with and for others, asking that specific needs be met through God's rich supply. But sometimes a friend's pain can be so great, or her circumstances so baffling and overwhelming, that we simply run out of words.

I told one such hurting friend that because I no longer knew how to pray for her, I would be holding her in a special place in my heart where every time God looked at me, the first thing He would see is her and her need.

This constant inner holding up of a dear one has proved to be one way I can love and support a friend and at the same time follow God's difficult command to "pray without ceasing" (1 Thessalonians 5:17). Such prayer is not a continual stream of words, but a silent and persistent keeping of the faith.

Many of our best prayers, in fact, are uttered without words. Some of our deepest petitions are groans, sighs, or tears salted with the pain of identification. Some of our most enduring entreaties are the silent leanings of the soul in trust—in the grateful knowledge that God is great, loving, and able. And some of our most effective prayers are poured out through active hands and feet, helping, carrying, lifting, and doing.

But whether we call on the Lord with or without words, we must keep calling! For some day we'll know what prayer is really worth—and we'll deeply regret that we prayed so little. But for now, we can be quite sure of this much: Our Father gathers our faithful, loving prayers and with such raw materials creates His marvelous answers.

"As for me, far be it from me that I should sin against the Lord by failing to pray for you."
—1 Samuel 12:23

And pray in the Spirit on all occasions with all kinds of prayers and requests. With this in mind, be alert and always keep on praying for all the saints.
—Ephesians 6:18

In the same way, the Spirit helps us in our weakness. We do not know what we ought to pray for, but the Spirit himself intercedes for us with groans that words cannot express. And he who searches our hearts knows the mind of the Spirit, because the Spirit intercedes for the saints in accordance with God's will.
—Romans 8:26–27

Blanket
People

Also, on a cold night, two under the same blanket gain warmth from each other, but how can one be warm alone?
—Ecclesiastes 4:11 TLB

This dear couple, Lord,
is like a cozy afghan
on a cool evening.
One has the wisdom of wool,
the other, warm color—
rich design.
I search for them when I'm
chilled,
and somehow with just a look,
a word, or a hug,
they wrap themselves snugly
about my heart.

I know now how it feels
to be embraced by You.

Some days we're burdened with such an inflated sense of failure and discouragement that we cannot even imagine God's arms opening wide enough to hold it all! We sit alone in the chill of our shortcomings and read in God's Word that Jesus said, "Come to me, all you who are weary and burdened" (Matthew 11:28).

Yet we cannot allow ourselves to be engulfed by His outstretched arms as He opened them on the cross . . . until a blanket person wraps us in acceptance and love by choosing to be near us when we would not even choose to be near ourselves.

God needs His blanket people, each with his or her unique color and design, each a demonstration of His warm, enfolding love.

Dear friends, let us love one another, for love comes from God. Everyone who loves has been born of God and knows God. Whoever does not love does not know God, because God is love. This is how God showed his love among us: He sent his one and only Son into the world that we might live through him.

*This is love: not that we loved God, but that He loved
us and sent his Son as an atoning sacrifice for our sins.
Dear friends, since God so loved us, we also ought to
love one another. We love because he first loved us.*

—1 John 4:7–11, 19

Time
Share

**"There is a time for everything, and a season for
every activity under heaven . . . "**
—Ecclesiastes 3:1

Among God's rich gifts to me are a twenty-four-hour
day and dear family and friends. Surely they were giv-
en to be spent on one another. But somehow that
doesn't always happen.

What is it that becomes more important than
people? Tasks? Duties? Schedules? Goals? These are
ever before us and do claim their rightful hours.

Yet how easily duty becomes greedy! How subtly
it taunts us with negligence if we spend time laughing, playing, and sharing with people.

Duty has a way (doesn't it?) of appearing more noble than time with friends or family. Duty manages to sit on a nerve and produce guilt if we don't produce an endless series of accomplishments. Thus it establishes our priorities.

So our dear ones wait. And we are all poorer in spirit and character for the lack of touching, helping, lifting, and shaping that we bring to one another.

Of course, duty deserves its proper due, but we need to remember that it dies with us. People don't.

I long to see you so that I may impart to you some spiritual gift to make you strong—that is, that you and I may be mutually encouraged by each other's faith. I do not want you to be unaware brothers, that I planned many times to come to you (but have been prevented from doing so until now) . . .
                                        —Romans 1:11–13

Let us consider how we may spur one another on toward love and good deeds. Let us not give up meeting together, as some are in the habit of doing, but let us encourage one another—and all the more as you see the Day approaching.   —Hebrews 10:24–25

The Trouble
With Change

Change is a threat to affection.
> —C. S. Lewis, *The Four Loves*

Occasionally when I'm walking out the door to go somewhere, my comedic son, Jeff, dramatically calls out after me, "Bye! Love you! Stay the same! Don't change!"

His playful affection always leaves me smiling and sometimes thinking. Does love have a tendency to resisit change? Is it disturbing to find a difference in someone we care for—especially when those differences alter her responses to us? Is the "predictable" preferable to the uncertainties of growth? Does any change, even positive change, make us feel uncomfortable, insecure?

Do we even resist making the choices and con-
structive behavioral changes necessary to our own
growth because we're unsure how we'll be received by
someone who has already demonstrated that she
accepts us just the way we are? Is change an assault to
affection?

Selfish affection may indeed seek the comfort of
the familiar at the expense of a loved one's progress.
But genuine love recognizes change as both the awesome responsibility and great privilege of close relationship. Real love encourages the transformation
that comes with maturing—even when my friend's
new patterns demand me to change in response. For
close relationship can both inspire and require
change in us.

As long-time friends, we have established a
"dance of relationship." I step forward and you step
back—now we whirl—now we dip—then you bend
backward to accommodate me, and I side-step the
real issue. But as you grow and change, your part in
our familiar pattern may be altered until your steps
no longer match mine.

Where you used to step back, always giving in to
my opinions and desires, you may begin to step forward with ideas and needs of your own. You may put

your foot down on an issue I've managed to avoid for years. If I can adjust my steps to match your new pattern of openness and confidence, our relationship is enriched with more variety and balance. If I cannot, or will not, allow you to grow, I will either back away or stumble on your healthy new assertiveness.

But as you have taken the risk of being true to the new person God is creating you to be our relationship is modified and, one way or another, I am changed. It is, after all, the life work of the Christian to be transformed until we look, act, and are like the Son of God.

When our relational challenges are choreographed by God, change can become a surprising new friend within our friendship. In Christ, we will find stability even in the constant challenges of our mutual transformation. Together our steps will move forward with grace until they match those of the Master.

You were taught, with regard to your former way of life, to put off your old self, which is being corrupted by its deceitful desires; to be made new in the attitude of your minds; and to put on the new self, created to be like God in true righteousness and holiness. There-

fore each of you must put off falsehood and speak truthfully to his neighbor, for we are all member of one body. —Ephesians 4:22-25

As iron sharpens iron, so one man [woman] sharpens another. —Proverbs 27:17

Built-in Strength

Not until our eyes are on the Lord will we be big enough to overlook differences and open enough to adapt and adjust.
   —Charles R. Swindoll, *Dropping Your Guard*

The sign on a billboard said, "Blessed are the flexible, for they shall not be bent out of shape."

How true, I thought, *and neither shall they be pulled and broken apart.* For in this changing world, flexibility is essential to survival.

Highways and bridges are designed to expand and contract in response to an ever-changing environment. Compression and tension members are built in to allow for the inevitable shifting brought on by temperature changes, heavy loads, and other stresses. Bridge-builders know that if these compression and tension members fail, so does the bridge.

When it comes to relationships, we must build into them as much adaptability as we can without sacrificing stability. The bridge between you and me remains strong only as we give, expand, and adjust. Relationships are never static; they are always growing or shrinking. Circumstances shift and alter. We view things differently. People move, change, and develop new interests and needs. Responsibilities and pressures fluctuate. The emotional climate heats up or cools down. Our spiritual condition changes.

What can we build into our friendships that will afford us the flexibility to survive it all? What can give us the resilience to stand strong through any storm, stress, struggle, or stagnation?

Only God's forgiving, grace-filled, patient, tender, committed, never-ending *love* offers us the flexibility and strength we need to stay together and stay strong in this stress-filled world. We love because He first loved us.

My purpose is that they may be encouraged in heart and united in love . , . —Colossians 2:2

God has poured out his love into our hearts by the Holy Spirit, whom he has given us.

—Romans 5:5

Love is patient, love is kind. It does not envy, it does not boast, it is not proud. It is not rude, it is not self seeking, it is not easily angered, it keeps no record of wrongs. Love does not delight in evil but rejoices with the truth, always hopes, always perseveres. Love never fails.   *—1 Corinthians 13:4–8*

Come to the Water

**He who has compassion on them will guide them
and lead them beside springs of water.**
—Isaiah 49:10

*If we could pause in our pursuit
to walk a sandy shore
and let our laughter
join the rhythm of God's waves . . .
If we could pitch smooth shells
at foaming surf and
fling feelings, hurl ideas,
and launch dreams . . .
If we could find a smooth gray rock
and sit in cozy silence while
crabs sidle by and
seagulls swoop from a cobalt sky . . .*

If we could pray with the
breeze tugging gently at our hair
and the sun warming
our clasped hands . . .
Then, my friend,
life's rushing tide would subside
leaving treasures of the deep
upon the sands of our souls.

The Lord will guide you always; he will satisfy your
needs in a sun-scorched land and will strengthen your
frame. You will be like a well-watered garden, like a
spring whose waters never fail.   —Isaiah 58:11

"Come, all you who are thirsty, come to the waters;
and you who have no money, come, buy and eat!
Come, buy wine and milk without money and without
cost. Why spend money on what is not bread and your
labor on what does not satisfy? Listen, listen to me,
and eat what is good, and your soul will delight in the
richest of fare."   —Isaiah 55:1–2

The Touch
of God

Jesus reached out his hand and touched . . .
—Matthew 8:3

Jesus,
I long to see You
face to face.
But for now
I love the way You
smile at me through
the face of a sister,
touch me with the hand of a child,
speak to me through
the voice of a brother,
care for me with the
heart of a friend.

I was at the drinking fountain, swallowing aspirin and complaining to my friend about my frequent headaches. She turned, put her arms around me, gave me a kiss on the cheek, and then simply said, "I love you."

Warm surprise told me I must have expected a sermonette on searching for causes, a dissertation on slowing down, a checklist of ten things for which to be thankful, or at the very least, "My, that is too bad," followed by a hasty exit.

Oh Lord, I thought, *maybe I expect you to preach at me too. How I wish you were so real, so present and understanding, that you could put your arms around me and dissolve my petty complaints with, "I love you."*

"My child, I can. I did. At the drinking fountain."

Today, Lord, You wrapped me in a warm hug. Maybe I can pass it on to somebody else with a headache, or a heartache.

"In just a little while I will be gone from the world, but I will still be present with you. For I will live again— and you will too. When I come back to life again, you will know that I am in my Father, and you in me, and I in you." —John 14:19–20

"And so I am giving a new commandment to you now—love each other just as much as I love you. Your strong love for each other will prove that you are my disciples."   —John 13:34–35 TLB

"Now that you know these things, you will be blessed if you do them."   —John 13:17

Devotional taken from *When the Handwriting on the Wall Is in Brown Crayon* by Susan Lenzkes, copyright © 1981.

Welded in Faithfulness

Many a man [woman] claims to have unfailing love, but a faithful man [woman] who can find?
—Proverbs 20:6

Many years ago a friend brought a newcomer to a group of which I was a part. As she presented each person in the circle, my friend gave that person's name followed by a brief introductory comment.

When she came to me, she said, "This is Susan." Then, laying her hand on my arm, she added, "and Susan is . . . faithful."

Faithful! You've got to be kidding, I thought. *Faithful?* I had the urge to wag my tail, roll over, and let her scratch my tummy!

In the ensuing years, however, I have come to consider her comment to be one of the highest compliments I could ever receive. Perhaps I didn't value it sufficiently at the time because I took faithfulness for granted. Faithfulness was part of my environmental inheritance; my parents had consistently modeled loyalty. It seemed the natural way to be.

But life soon taught me that faithfulness is not natural to many people. It is natural only to those who are spirit-filled, to those who have inherited it as a fruit of the Spirit from the heavenly Father.

We serve a trustworthy God. What He says He will do, He *does*. What He promises, He *delivers*. When He says He'll be with us always, He *is*. His is no love on velcro strips, but love that sticks and *stays*. You can build a solid relationship on that kind of faithfulness. We His children need to follow His example.

Do our friends know they can count on us to keep our word? To keep on loving them no matter what? To see the good in them even when they can't? To hold onto them when they've let go? And to let them grow, even if it seems to be away from us?

Such faithfulness will be the welding that holds our bridges of friendship together in solid, committed, eternal love.

Love and faithfulness meet together; righteousness and peace kiss each other. —Psalm 85:10

The Lord is faithful to all his promises and loving toward all he has made. —Psalm 145:13

Let love and faithfulness never leave you; bind them around your neck, write them on the tablet of your heart. Then you will win favor and a good name in the sight of God and man. —Proverbs 3:3–4

My eyes will be on the faithful in the land, that they may dwell with me. —Psalm 101:6

A Final Word

I *already knew* the importance of friends when I started writing this book. In fact, I'd been itching to write a book about friendship for years. But by the time I finished this manuscript, God had given me more reminders of the immeasurable value of friends than I had ever hoped to need.

It all started right after my friends helped ease me past the half century mark on my calendar. I figured that was quite enough trauma for one summer, but I was wrong.

The day after my birthday our daughter, Cathy, and her husband, Wes, had to move in with us to escape a crazed, dangerous, threatening new tenant in their apartment complex where she is the manager. Later that week the implant that had been in Cathy's hip for only three years broke loose, gouging painfully into her bone. To prevent further damage, she was confined to bed, unable to move. Her medical insurance wouldn't cover treatment because her problem was a pre-existing condition. Friends prayed and worked with us seeking ways to fund her urgently needed surgery while I cared for her around the clock. We're sick of bedpans now.

During this time my husband, Herb, received his lay-off notice from his job in the declining aerospace industry. He was also spending increasingly more days in bed with back pain after a fall at work. A flight of stairs separated my two immobilized patients. Friends prayed, sent encouraging notes, called to see what they could do to help. "Send anything but an exercise machine," I responded.

Our daughter was finally admitted for surgery—a total hip replacement this time. The day she came home from the hospital and settled into her bed, we discovered that Herb could no longer get out of his. An emergency MRI the next morning revealed multiple abnormalities on his spine. The doctor said, "What we're seeing has nothing to do with that work accident we've been treating him for. I'm sorry, but it looks like . . . cancer."

We were in shock. A week of testing revealed that Herb was in the most advanced stage of prostate cancer. "He's way too young for this!" doctors said. The disease had metastasized throughout his entire skeletal structure. That explained the terrible, spreading back pain.

We went away with our children to cry, hold one another, talk, and face death. But within days Herb had to be hospitalized to control the pain and to see what could be done. We settled on a treatment plan and, after a week, Herb, along with several bags of medicine, came home.

During this time friends surrounded us, wept with us, called us, sent notes, gathered information, brought food, ran errands, cleaned our house, prayed with us, and believed for us. One friend even brought a delicious full-course dinner, balloons, and presents for Herb's fifty-fourth birthday when we were too numb to celebrate.

And there were other signs of divine help. Herb's employer removed him from lay-off status and put him on disability so he could keep his insurance benefits. Wes's employer relieved him from extensive travel obligations so he could care for Cathy. The doctors and hospitals agreed to significantly reduce their fees for Cathy's surgery and to accept monthly payments rather than demand immediate remuneration, as their policy stated. God had His friends everywhere.

Cathy is healing now and getting around on crutches. And Herb, praise God, seems to be going into remission. We don't know how much time God will allow him, but we do know that we could not have made it this far without the help of the loving Friend who promises never to leave us. And then there are those precious people we are privileged to call friends.

Gather them while you can.

Note to the Reader

The publisher invites you to share your response to the message of this book by writing Discovery House Publishers, P.O. Box 3566, Grand Rapids, MI 49501, U.S.A. or by calling 1-8 00-653-8333. For information about other Discovery House publications, contact us at the same address and phone number.